CALUMET CITY PUBLIC LIBRARY

3 1613 00517 8010

W9-BUU-587

THE AMAZING HUMAN BODY

The Eyes Have It

J
612.84
EYE
0.25

0415 #28× 10/12

CALUMET CITY PUBLIC
LIBRARY

**Edited by
Joanne Randolph**

Enslow Publishing
101 W. 23rd Street
Suite 240
New York, NY 10011
USA

enslow.com

This edition published in 2018 by:
Enslow Publishing, LLC.
101 W. 23rd Street, Suite 240
New York, NY 10011

Additional materials copyright © 2018 by Enslow Publishing, LLC

All rights reserved.

No part of this book may be reproduced in any form without permission in writing from the publisher.

Library of Congress Cataloging-in-Publication Data

Names: Randolph, Joanne, editor.
Title: The eyes have it / edited by Joanne Randolph.
Description: New York, NY : Enslow Publishing, 2018. | Series: The amazing human body | Audience: Grade level 5-8. | Includes
  bibliographical references and index.
Identifiers: LCCN 2017001871| ISBN 9780766089938 (pbk. book) | ISBN 9780766089952 (library bound book) | ISBN
  9780766089945 (6 pack)
Subjects: LCSH: Vision—Juvenile literature.
Classification: LCC QP475.7 .E94 2018 | DDC 612.8/4—dc23
LC record available at https://lccn.loc.gov/2017001871

Printed in China

To Our Readers: We have done our best to make sure all website addresses in this book were active and appropriate when we went to press. However, the author and the publisher have no control over and assume no liability for the material available on those websites or on any websites they may link to. Any comments or suggestions can be sent by email to customerservice@enslow.com.

Photos Credits: Cover, p. 1 SpeedKingz/Shutterstock.com; ksenia_bravo/Shutterstock.com (series logo); p. 3, back cover Tusiy/ Shutterstock.com; pp. 4, 12, 21, 28, 36 Sergey Nivens/Shutterstock.com (digital eye art), SUWIT NGAOKAEW/Shutterstock. com (chemical structure background); p. 5 rendix_alextian/Shutterstock.com; p. 6 Peter Hermes Furian/Alamy Stock Photo; p. 8 Alila Medical Media/Shutterstock.com; p. 10 Atypeek/DigitalVision Vectors/Getty Images; p. 13 Brad Sauter/Shutterstock.com; p. 14 Spencer Sutton/Science Source/Getty Images; p. 16 Dept. Of Clinical Cytogenetics, Addenbrookes Hospital/Science Photo Library/Getty Images; p. 18 Wision/Shutterstock.com; p. 22 Prof. P. Motta/Dept. Of Anatomy/University La Sapienza/Rome/ Science Photo Library/Getty Images; p. 23 udaix/Shutterstock.com; p. 24 Doug Perrine/Perspectives/Getty Images; p. 26 Stuart Dee/Photographer's Choice/Getty Images; p. 29 Tomatito/Shutterstock.com; p. 30 Laguna Design/Science Photo Library/Getty Images; pp. 32-33 ERproductions Ltd/Blend Images/Getty Images; pp. 34-35 Monkey Business Images/Shutterstock.com; p. 37 Matthew Leete/DigitalVision/Getty Images; p. 38 Science Source; p. 39 Alila Medical Media/Shutterstock.com; pp. 40-41 gilaxia/ E+/Getty Images; pp. 42-43 Philippe Psaila/Science Source.

Article Credits: Ellen R. Braaf, "Do We See with Our Eyes or Brain?" *Ask;* Stephen James O'Meara, "What Color Is a Fire Engine?" *Odyssey;* Nick D'Alto, "The 'See' Horse," *Odyssey;* Rani Iyer, "Don't Believe Your Eyes: The Science of Sight," *Odyssey;* Nick D'Alto, "Second Sight: Glimpsing the Future of Bionic Vision," *Odyssey.*

All articles © by Carus Publishing Company. Reproduced with permission.

All Cricket Media material is copyrighted by Carus Publishing Company, d/b/a Cricket Media, and/or various authors and illustrators. Any commercial use or distribution of material without permission is strictly prohibited. Please visit http://www. cricketmedia.com/info/licensing2 for licensing and http://www.cricketmedia.com for subscriptions.

CONTENTS

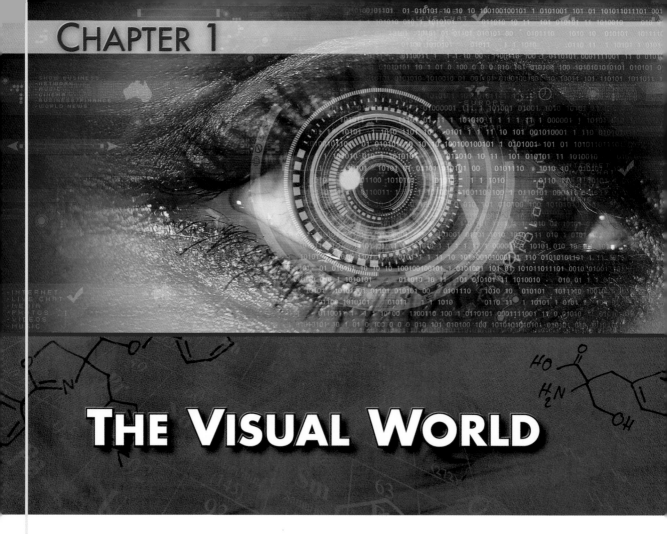

CHAPTER 1

THE VISUAL WORLD

Your eyes and brain form a visual system. This means they work together to let you see and experience the world in your own special way.

So let's say it's a bright, sunny morning. You're walking in a barnyard and come across a creature called Stinky sitting in a pen. Light rays from the sun bounce off Stinky and stream toward you in straight lines.

Your eye is a fluid-filled ball. It sits in a bony eye socket in the front of your skull. There's a clear part that covers the front of your eyeball. It's your cornea, which acts like a lens to bend the light rays that carry Stinky's image. Stinky's image passes to the colored part of your eye. This part is called the iris. The image continues on through the pupil, a black dot that's just an empty space like the hole in a doughnut. It then reaches the clear structure behind the pupil. This is called the lens. This lens finishes the bending process.

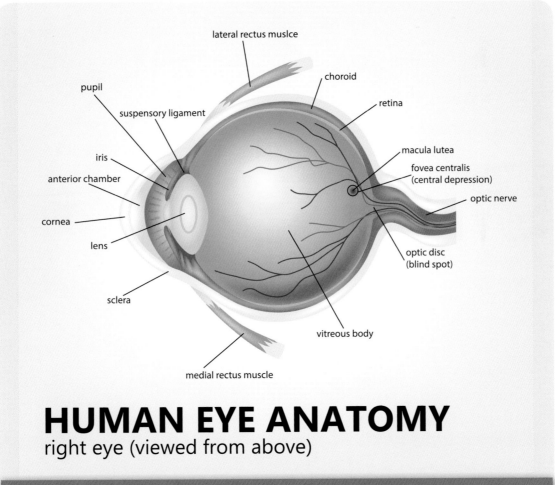

lateral rectus muslce
choroid
pupil
retina
suspensory ligament
macula lutea
iris
fovea centralis (central depression)
anterior chamber
optic nerve
cornea
lens
optic disc (blind spot)
sclera
vitreous body
medial rectus muscle

HUMAN EYE ANATOMY
right eye (viewed from above)

This diagram shows the many parts that make up the human eye, such as the cornea, the lens, and the retina.

It also focuses the light so that Stinky's image will strike the retina at just the right place. The retina's job is to catch light. Stinky's image is now the size of a postage stamp. Plus, as a result of all that bending, it is upside down!

The upside-down image is changed into electrical and chemical signals. These signals zip along the optic nerve. The optic nerve travels

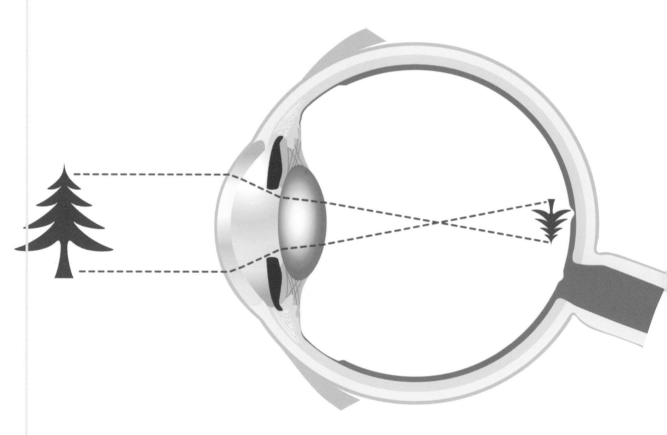

This diagram helps illustrate how the curved lens of the eye bends the light, which results in the image hitting the back of the eye upside down.

from the back of each eyeball to the brain. Other nerves then bring the signals to the back of the brain. Here your brain puts all the raw data it receives together and forms a right-side-up image of Stinky.

So when you say "I see Stinky, the pig," you're really talking about your vision, not your sight. Your eyes don't know what a pig is. It's your brain that makes sense of the images sent to it.

DO WE SEE WITH OUR EYES OR BRAIN?

Mike May had been on airplanes lots of times. But two years ago, he took a flight to Los Angeles he'll remember all his life. He looked out the window. He then turned to a lady sitting next to him and said, "Excuse me, I just got my sight back last week after being totally blind for 43 years. Could you help me figure out what I'm seeing?" The woman just stared. Mike broke the awkward silence and asked if the white lines he saw in the distance were mountains. "No, honey," the lady said in amazement, "that's haze." For the rest of the trip, the lady and her husband gave Mike a "play-by-play" of all they passed.

It's easy to take sight for granted. Have you ever stopped to think about all the different things you're able to see? Think about the colors in a rainbow, patterns on a butterfly's wing, huge skyscrapers, and tiny grains of sand. You can see the words on this page and faraway stars. You can watch a fuzzy caterpillar crawl along a leaf and sleek racecars zoom around a track. You can see your coach's hand signals and your best friend's smile.

Your eyes help you to know the world around you. But they don't do the job alone. As optometrist Dr. Arthur Seiderman reminds his patients, "Sight occurs in the eyes. Vision is the interplay between the eyes and the brain."

The Visual Projection Pathway

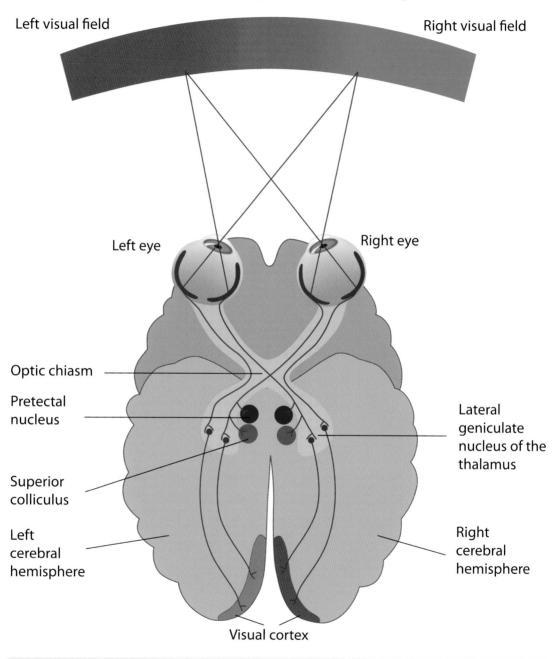

This diagram shows the visual projection pathway, or how the information from your eyes gets to the visual cortex of the brain.

Every second you're awake, your eyes send new data to your brain. In fact, they send more than a billion pieces! Your brain makes sense out of what you see. From 70 to 80 percent of the information you gather reaches you through your eyes. That's why sight is considered your most important or dominant sense.

The day you were born, you just opened your eyes and you could "see." But what you saw was a blurred world of light and dark patterns. In the "classroom" of your crib, you taught yourself to focus your eyes on objects that were both near and far, and to follow a moving object. You had to learn that you could move your eyes without moving your whole head, that your hands and feet were parts of your own body, and you learned to recognize the faces of the people around you. You quickly learned to separate the figures you were looking at from their backgrounds. When it comes to making visual memories, you were—and still are—a creative genius.

Blind people who have gained their sight or partial sight—especially if they were blind from birth—have no visual memories of the world. They have to learn to make sense out of what they are seeing, just like a newborn baby. Mike May was three years old when he lost his sight due to an accident. But he went to public school, played sports, attended college and graduate school, married, had two children, and became a champion skier who holds the world speed record for downhill skiing by a blind person. Through a miracle of surgery, Mike's sight has been restored, yet he still has trouble with his vision because his brain has never been programmed to process the visual information sent to it by his eyes.

The challenge that lies ahead for Mike is to learn to sort and process all the raw data sent to his brain from his eyes so he can more fully experience the visual word.

Optical illusions can be created by using different patterns and colors.
This circular optical illusion looks like it is moving!

OPTICAL ILLUSIONS: FOOLING YOUR BRAIN

When you see, your brain puts together many pieces of information. What happens is really very complicated. Sometimes your brain can get confused.

For instance, each eye has a slightly different view of the world or field of vision. Your brain, using information from both eyes, puts these slightly different views together to make a three-dimensional mind picture.

But you can fool your brain. Roll up a piece of white paper to form a tube. With your right eye, look through that tube at a distant object. While you're staring off into the distance, place your left hand—palm facing toward you—alongside the tube about 5 inches (13 centimeters) from your nose, so the edge of your left hand rests against the tube. With both eyes open, stare off into the distance. Can you see a hole in your hand?

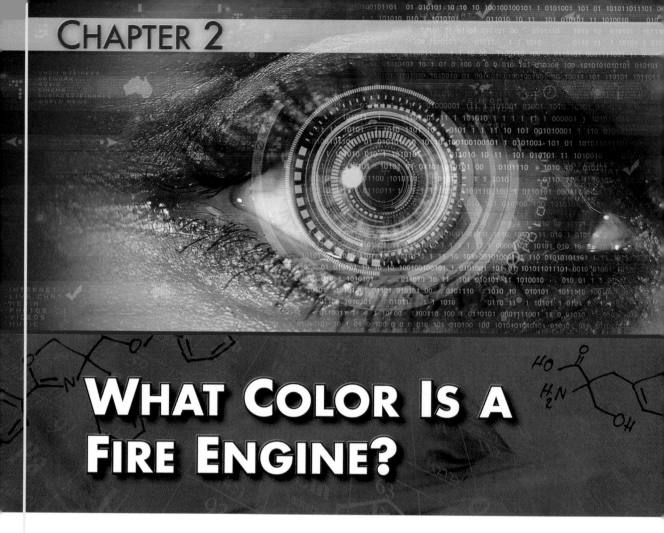

CHAPTER 2

WHAT COLOR IS A FIRE ENGINE?

f you're a person with normal color vision, you no doubt reply, "Red, silly!" But if you're one of ten million or more Americans who are color deficient, the answer is not at all obvious. What is red?

Color vision isn't "black and white" in more ways than one. When you look at a red fire engine, how do you know it's the same color red that someone else sees? The fact is, tests of color vision have shown that no one sees color in exactly the same way. In most instances, the differences are subtle. But some people's color vision is quite different from the norm. These people are color vision deficient. This condition is sometimes called "color blindness." It's rare to find someone who sees no color at all, though.

Most of us see a fire engine as red in color, but not everyone sees color in the same way.

EYE-SCREAM CONES

When it comes to color, what we see isn't necessarily what we get. The end result depends on the condition of our eyes' color receptors. These are called cone cells because of what they look like under a microscope. Cone cells (or cones) are located in the retina—the layer of cells that line the innermost part of the eye. They work best in daylight. Each one contains a pigment that's sensitive to one of the three primary colors of light: red, green, and blue. People with normal color vision then have trichromatic (three-color) vision. Incoming light stimulates one or more of the eye's cone cells. Color

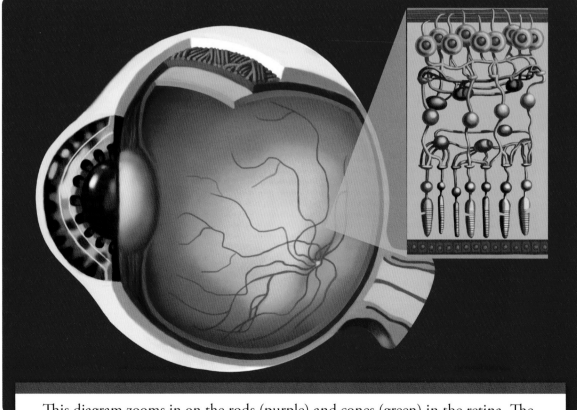

This diagram zooms in on the rods (purple) and cones (green) in the retina. The rods respond to dim light, enabling images to be detected. Cones detect color. The rods and cones pass visual signals through the optic nerve to the brain.

is the result of information coming from the three color receptors, each of which is stimulated to a different extent.

In most cases of color deficiency, the eyes have a normal number of cone cells. However, one of the visual pigments may not be working well, or is missing. People with this condition have dichromatic (two-color) vision. More than 95 percent of all variations in human color vision involve the red and green receptors. This means most dichromatic people have trouble distinguishing reds from greens. (The level of trouble depends on how properly the cones are functioning.) A much less common form of color deficiency is blue-yellow. People have more difficulty seeing color if one of the cone types is missing entirely or does not function at all.

IT'S IN THE GENES

Some 10 percent of males of European origin and about one-half of one percent of females experience some amount of dichromatic color vision. The figure varies with people of other origins. The reason for this curious discrepancy in gender has to do with heredity. The gene for the deficiency is carried on the X chromosome. Males have only one X chromosome, while females have two. Therefore, color deficiencies can occur much more easily in males and are typically passed to them by their mothers. A color-deficient father can only pass the gene to his daughters. They will have normal color vision unless their mother also carries the color-deficient gene. Color-deficient vision may also be caused by disease of the optic nerve or by a malfunctioning retina.

The most common form of color deficiency is deuteranopia. This is when the eye's cones are poor receptors of green light. While

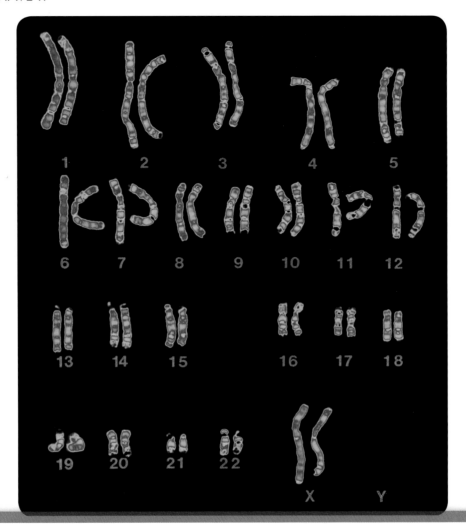

Each human cell has forty-six chromosomes that hold the information for things such as the ability to see color. These chromosomes belong to a female because there are two X chromosomes.

people with deuteranopia probably cannot see reds and greens in the same way that color-normal people can, they can often distinguish between shades of red and green relatively accurately. Someone with this condition may not be aware that they have color-deficient vision until they take an eye test. People whose cones are deficient in, or insensitive to, red light have protanopia. To them, red looks more like dark yellow or beige, while green looks like red. It's very rare for anyone to be "blind" to the blue end of the spectrum (tritanopia). An extremely small minority of people have monochromacy, where the cone cells fail to function; people with this condition are truly color blind, seeing the world like an old black-and-white movie.

LIFE IN DICHROMATIC COLOR

While it's a myth that most people with color-deficient vision see the world in black and white, they are faced with color challenges. Perhaps the most important is how to respond to a traffic light. If you can't tell the difference between red and green, how do you know whether to stop or go? Actually, the answer is simple. In most states, traffic lights are oriented with red on the top and green at the bottom. So if a color-deficient person sees the bottom light illuminate, he knows it's OK to proceed. People with dichromatic vision do have problems, however, when they enter a city or state where traffic lights are horizontal. More of a problem is the single caution light: Is it red or yellow?

Other simple pleasures in life become somewhat confusing. For instance, imagine trying to color match your clothes without help, or paint a rich autumn landscape. Some dichromates have trouble eating certain foods because of the way they look. Spinach, for instance, can look like cow droppings. Children can be ridiculed for coloring an ocean red, or a person with green hair. A red-green color deficient friend cannot appreciate a stunning sunset with intense red clouds and a rare, blue moon.

HOW COLORFUL ARE YOUR CONES?

How do you know if your cones are up to snuff? Your doctor tests you for color deficiencies. Don't worry, you most likely have normal color vision. But remember, not everyone sees color the same way. So the shade of color that you see is unique to you.

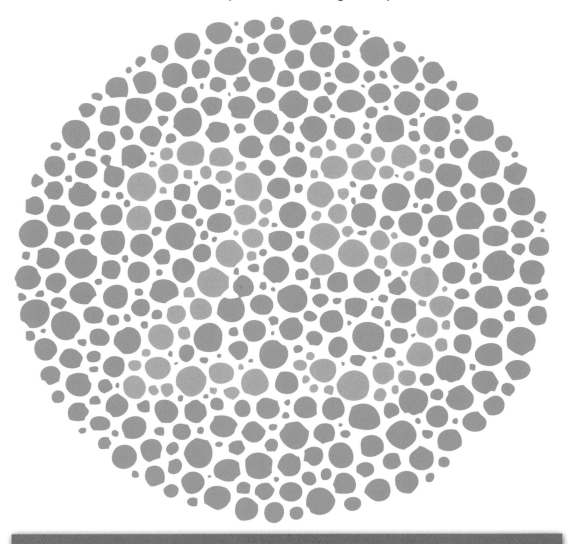

This is a test for color blindness. If you can see the number in the circle, you are not color blind!

SIMULATING COLOR BLINDNESS

Many website pictures and graphics are difficult for color-blind people to view. The Vischeck website allows you to open your eyes to the world of color blindness. Choose any standard image files on your computer and have Vischeck show you how they would look to someone with one of three different types of color-deficient vision. You can also check out their examples. Check it out at http://www.vischeck.com/examples/.

HOW DOES PISTACHIO ICE CREAM TASTE? GREEN!

When is a sound not a sound? When you're a synesthete, because then it's also a shape, a color, a scent, and a taste. Synesthetes are people with a statistically rare medical condition called synesthesia. Just as "anesthesia" refers to the partial or complete loss of a sensation, synesthesia refers to a joined sensation. When a synesthete hears a sound, she might also see a specific color associated with the pitch of that sound, detect its scent, or both. A highly sensitive synesthete might experience a union of all five senses—touch, smell, hearing, taste, and sight.

If a synesthete, for instance, hears a chugging train, he or she also might see blue blobs, lines, or spirals, feel smooth textures, or sense a salty taste in his or her mouth. Colors appear to flash in front of their eyes as if projected on a screen just inches away. Not all synesthetes, however, will see or feel the same sensations when they hear the chugging train. One synesthete might see periwinkle blue, while another sees forest green or lemon yellow. But each individual's experience will remain constant and consistent over a lifetime.

Many American non-synesthetes experience a bit of what it's like to be a synesthete every New Year's Eve and July Fourth. When you experience a colorful explosion of fireworks set to the bombastic musical finale of Tchaikovsky's 1812 Overture, you see colors explode as you hear the music swell and fade.

Synesthesia is an involuntary brain process. It's not something that an individual can control. It just happens, like a headache, or when you see "silverfish" swimming before your eyes. Females and left-handed people are more likely to have synesthesia than are their counterparts, and it also runs in families.

Richard Cytowic, MD, a neurologist who's spent many years studying the condition, says that about one in twenty-five thousand may have it, but the exact number is unknown. In fact, Cytowic argues that we may all have the condition but are not aware of its presence. Children are also more synesthetic than adults. Cytowic says there's evidence that some children lose their synesthesia between ages eleven and thirteen, around the time of puberty. Hormonal changes in the brain might affect a person's awareness of the condition.

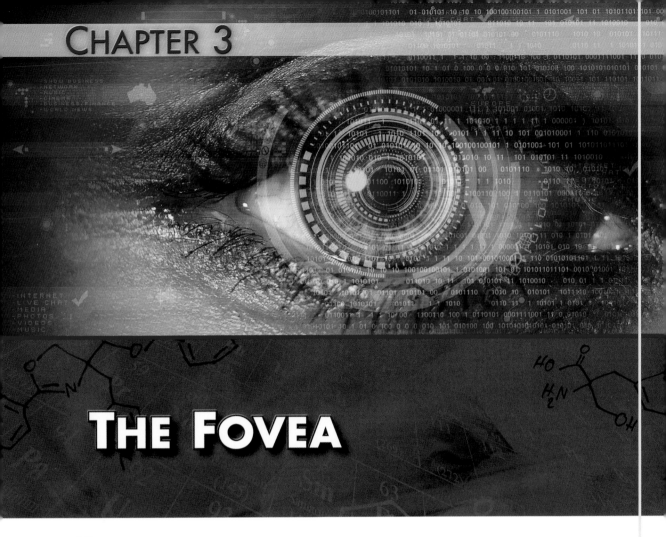

CHAPTER 3

THE FOVEA

This sea horse has its eye on you—literally. A sea horse can move both eyes independently, keeping one on its prey, while tracking a predator with the other. Add superb color vision, and the sea horse enjoys a remarkable view of its world. But what's more surprising is that these ocean creatures see in one way that's remarkably like us.

"Sea horse eyes contain foveas," explains Dr. Keely Bumsted O'Brien, a lead researcher at Australia's Centre of Excellence in Vision Science. Foveas are rare among us mammals; only humans and other primates have them. They're also tiny. The foveas in your eyes are smaller than the head of a pin. Nevertheless, you couldn't see without them.

21

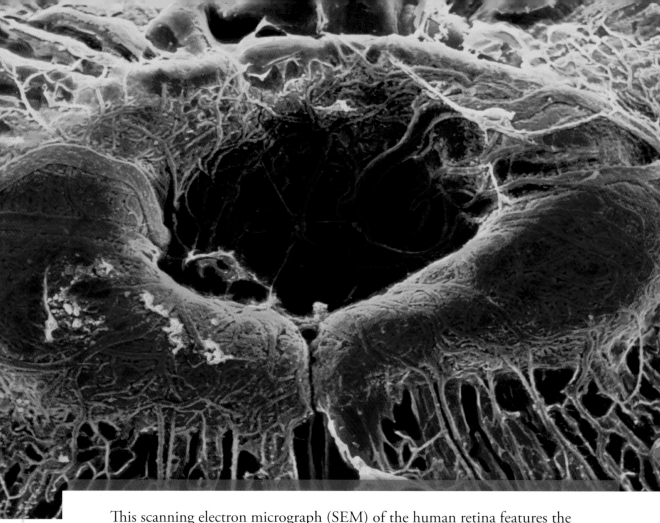

This scanning electron micrograph (SEM) of the human retina features the central fovea, a craterlike depression in the photosensitive layer of the eye.

Foveas work like the HDTV of human vision: they deliver the highest-quality picture. This tiny pit (fovea is Latin for "a pit") at the center of each retina contains more than two hundred thousand cones (the cells that give us color vision) in each square millimeter. "This dense concentration of cones lets the fovea pick up fine detail," Bumsted O'Brien says. The fovea is located within the retina's macula. That's the part of the eye that provides us with clear, central vision. Surrounding parts of the retina, which provide peripheral (at the edges) vision, see less sharply. They're better at noticing shapes and shadows.

You just used your foveas to read this sentence, but in a surprising way. "When we read or look at a scene," observes Bumsted O'Brien, "it seems as if we see everything with equal clarity. But our eyes really see only a bit of it sharply, the part that falls on our foveas. To see everything clearly, our eyes are always moving." These eye movements are called saccades (suh-CODs). They're so tiny and rapid that we never notice them.

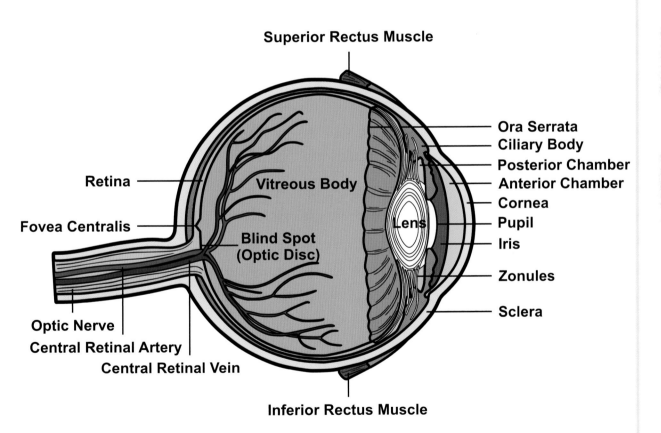

An illustration of the eye shows its structure, including the optic nerve, the retina, as well as the fovea, labeled the "fovea centralis" on the left in the diagram.

Of course sea horses don't read books. But how they use their foveas is equally fascinating. "Sea horses are ambush predators," Bumsted O'Brien says. "They eat very small, fast-moving crustaceans. They use their foveas to see their prey in fine detail." The Australian team tracked sea horses' eyes as they hunted inside a specially prepared tank. Video footage recorded when the animals' eyes moved to "lock onto" their prey. The team also studied the structure of the eyes themselves. "Sea horse foveas aren't exactly like ours," the scientist says. "However, both exhibit a very high density of cones."

This similarity is important, because human foveas develop their cone density over time, improving how we see. "Pediatricians know that youngsters can't see fine detail until about age five," Bumsted O'Brien notes. But how the fine-tuning vision process occurs is

Sea horses are one of the few animals to have foveas.

difficult to study in humans. Now, the Australian team's findings confirm that young sea horses also lack visual acuity. In behavioral tests, young sea horses could catch (see) only larger prey, suggesting their foveas also improve with maturity.

Studying sea horse eyes in this way may help scientists better understand how human vision develops, which could help doctors better treat abnormalities of the eye, as well as repair injuries. It offers particular promise for patients who suffer from macular degeneration, a disease in which the human fovea deteriorates, in extreme cases robbing victims of their sight. "If we can better understand how sea horse foveas develop," Bumsted O'Brien concludes, "we may, in the future, be able to use that knowledge to regenerate human foveas for these patients."

THE MIND'S EYE

The fovea occupies just one percent of our visual field. Yet it provides 50 percent of the visual information that our eyes send to our brain. Like electrical wiring, each cone in the fovea has its own nerve fiber running directly to the brain.

MONA LISA OF THE SEA HORSES

Why does the expression of the figure in the famous Leonardo da Vinci painting, *Mona Lisa*, seem to change? Turns out it's all in your foveas. Harvard University vision expert Dr. Margaret Livingstone has noted that da Vinci painted the smile of his *Mona Lisa* using carefully blended shadows. We see shadows best

3 1613 00517 8010

CALUMET CITY PUBLIC LIBRARY

The *Mona Lisa* is famous for her mysterious smile. Da Vinci painted the Mona Lisa in 1503. Today it is on display in the Louvre, a museum in Paris.

from the corners of our eyes. Look straight on, and the lady's smile vanishes. This is because our central vision (our foveal area) sees detail, not shadows, best. An expert anatomist, da Vinci studied the subtleties of human vision, and used them to make the woman in his painting seem alive. What would a sea horse see? Maybe beauty really is in the "eye" of the beholder.

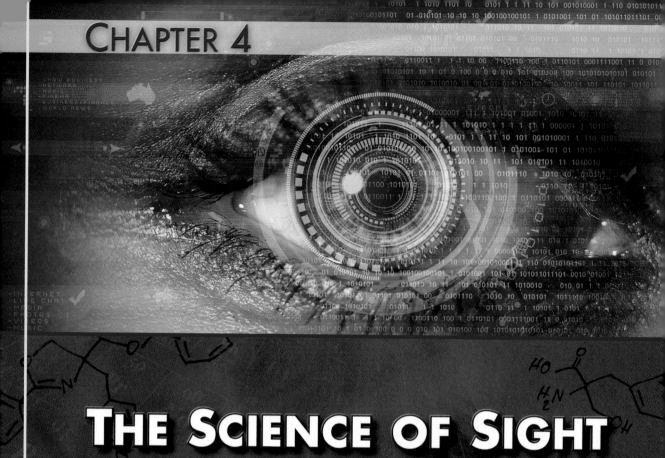

CHAPTER 4

THE SCIENCE OF SIGHT

Our eyes act like a camera. They capture images from the world around us. The images can be individual objects or the features of the setting we are located in. Our eyes also help us to identify the vivid color of an object—a rose or an apple—from the surrounding background. Looking at the rose, we can guess how far it is from us. Our eyes can also discern the texture and other features of the flower. We do all this automatically, without thinking about it.

MORE THAN A CAMERA

But a neuroscientist will explain that a human eye is more than a camera. It not only captures images but also transmits and interprets these images. An eye is a complicated organ despite its simple structure. Some organisms possess light-sensitive cells clustered together, known as "simple eyes." Such eyes can distinguish light and dark, but they can't detect objects or images. However, even simple eyes require an extremely complex mechanism to support vision. In fact, human eyes are considered simple eyes, too. This means there is only one lens. Some animals have compound eyes with more than one lens.

Insects, such as this fly, have compound eyes. Humans, in contrast, have simple eyes, which, despite the name, are in fact quite complicated.

BEHIND THE SCENES

The process of vision begins when photons, or bits of light, are first sensed by the eye. This happens in a specialized molecule called 11-cis-retinal. Just as ice changes when exposed to heat, the molecule that captures the photon also changes its shape and structure. This new molecule is called a rhodopsin. The energy of the photon continues to change the rhodopsin. It too becomes a new molecule. The new shape and structure is called metarhodopsin II.

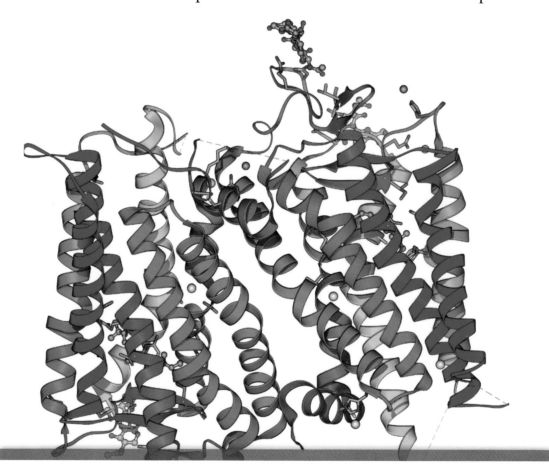

The rhodopsin molecule almost looks like a bunch of strands of curling ribbon. Without rhodopsin, we would not be able to see in dim light.

This shape is a perfect fit, like a piece in a jigsaw puzzle, for a gap in a giant protein. Next, this protein picks up several other molecules and becomes a long chain. This long chain is composed of living molecules that are constantly reacting with each other. A series of chemical reactions in this chain causes an electric current to be sent to the brain. When the brain interprets this current, it results in vision. All these chemical reactions take place at tremendous speed. It also requires a lot of energy. It is metabolically very expensive to maintain vision.

THE EYE-BRAIN CONNECTION

When we watch television or movies, we see images moving continuously on a screen. But, actually, there is a gap in the images. The continuity is an optical illusion. The optic nerve in our eye responds to changes in light about ten times every second. When the optic nerve is "resetting," images are not registered as separate objects. Because of this, when we view objects in rapid succession, the eye identifies fixed images as moving and continuous.

The retina is basically a part of the brain. It sends about ten million bits of information per second to the visual cortex region in the brain. The optical nerve pauses between the images, causing a small gap between them. The brain fills in the gaps by using the information received just fractions of seconds before. These images could be from a different distance or angle. Our eyes and brain function together to fill the gap in the information received. This compensation enables the impression of a smooth movie-like stream.

READING THE IMAGES

When we use binoculars, we sometimes see two slightly different images of the scene from each eyepiece. Similarly, eyes record two different aspects of images. When we focus the binoculars, the separate images merge. Our brain does this for us. This difference in vision is known as "binocular disparity."

Our brains fill in the gaps of what we are looking at through binoculars.

The difference between the images from both eyes serves an important purpose. Because the images are not really perfect copies of each other, it helps the brain figure out the depth of any scene. Light, shade, shadows, color, and relative sizes of objects all add to perception of depth. By manipulating any of these factors, moviemakers enrich the viewer's experience.

WHAT ABOUT 3-D MOVIES?

Movies that are 2-D and 3-D are both projected on a flat screen. But they are made and projected differently. A 3-D movie is recorded using two different cameras, placed side by side, to capture slightly different images. The image for the left eye is captured using horizontally polarized light— light that comes from a single direction. The images for the right eye are captured in vertically polarized light. To play the movie on the screen, two projectors simultaneously display separate images for the left eye and right eye. These images are superimposed on the screen.

Special 3-D glasses allow us to watch 3-D movies and see all the special effects.

Our brain puts the images together. Yet, because of the speed of display, the images on the screen will be blurred. This is corrected by wearing special glasses. Recall that the images for the left eye are captured using polarized light. The glasses add one more dimension to our viewing experience. They have a filter that blocks all wavelengths except the red light spectrum for the left eye. Similarly, 3-D glasses have a cyan (blue) filter for the right eye. The images for the left eye are projected horizontally, while the images for the right eye are projected vertically. This is similar to weaving cloth using threads in both the horizontal and vertical plane. The glasses with polarizing filters help our eyes "see" and our brain "experience" the different objects projected on the screen.

Three-dimensional movies may be fun, but they're not perfect. Some viewers experience headache, nausea, or even convulsions while watching them. Scientists and moviemakers are working to improve our movie-going experience by understanding more about the eye-brain connection.

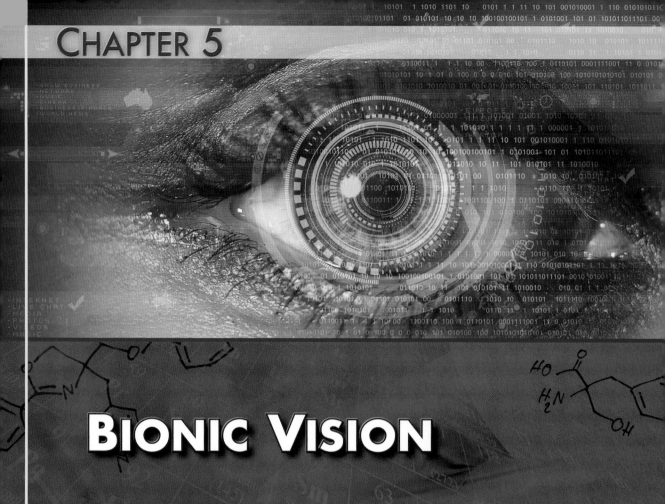

CHAPTER 5

BIONIC VISION

I magine: a young woman is walking along the beach ahead of you. She's wearing sunglasses and has an iPod-like device in her shirt pocket (a fine wire leads up to her face). She looks just like any other beachcomber enjoying the ocean view. But there's a difference: this sightseer is legally blind.

The young woman's sunglasses conceal a tiny video camera that relays imagery to artificial retinas implanted in her eyes. What looks like her iPod is really the device's power supply. Labs around the world are developing bionic eyes like hers. They will soon offer the possibility of sight for some special kinds of blindness.

Is this woman just listening to her music player or is she seeing the world for the first time? Bionic vision allows some people who are legally blind to enjoy some sight. So far, the technology does not allow for full-color vision, but it's a start!

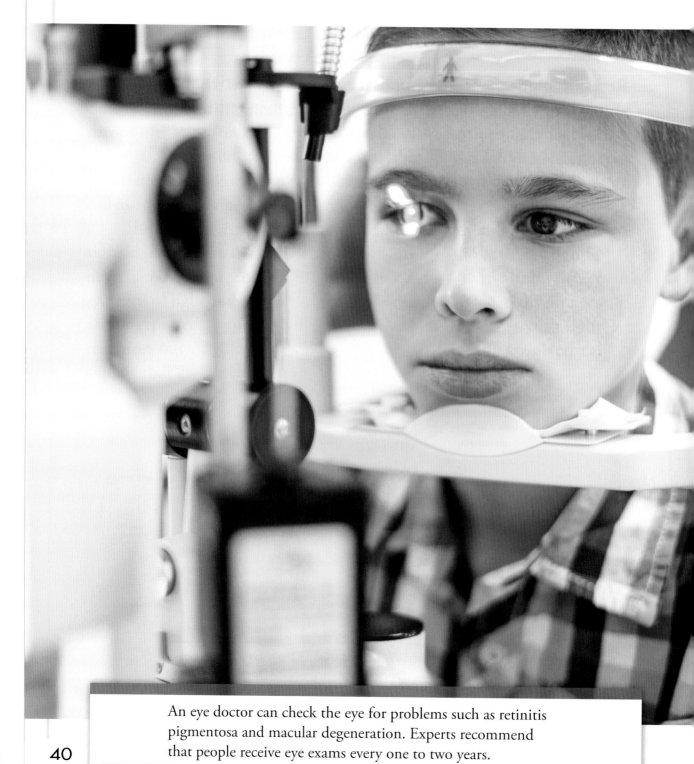

An eye doctor can check the eye for problems such as retinitis pigmentosa and macular degeneration. Experts recommend that people receive eye exams every one to two years.

In many patients, however, the other parts of the visual system all remain healthy. So while these patients' eyes can no longer see, their brains potentially can. Researchers hope to restore their vision by finding a way to bypass damaged eye tissues. Their hope is to deliver "electrical sight" directly to their nerves and brains.

RADIO VISION

Specialists at the Boston Retinal Implant Project range from neuroscientists to electrical engineers. They are working together to create a bionic vision system like the one described earlier. (The project is a collaboration of the Massachusetts Institute of Technology [MIT], Harvard Medical School, the Massachusetts Eye and Ear Infirmary, and the Department of Veterans Affairs.) Dr. Shawn Kelly, a visiting scientist at MIT and Electrical Engineering Research Manager on the project, explains how the system, currently under development, will operate.

"Instead of seeing light with their eyes, patients will rely on a tiny video camera, mounted to a pair of glasses," says Kelly. "[The system] will perform the first function of healthy [eyes]—it will capture a visual image of the world."

A processor in the glasses will turn what the camera sees into radio signals. A tiny antenna will transmit the information wirelessly. A second antenna, a coil of fine gold wire, will be implanted around the patient's eyeball. This will catch signals similar to the way an ordinary radio works. More gold wires will connect the coil to a microchip. This will be attached to the side of the eyeball. The microchip will act as a computer to understand the signals and activate an array of tiny electrodes. These electrodes take on the job of the rods and cones.

"These electrodes perform the second function of healthy rods and cones—they transmit electrical impulses into [the eye's] nerve endings," says Kelly. "From there, the signals will excite the appropriate areas of the brain, creating the sensation of vision."

Determining how many electrodes are needed to provide useful vision is a key design goal for the researchers. "A healthy retina contains over 100 million rods and cones, but early testing suggests as few as 15 electrodes can produce recognizable shapes," says Kelly. "The image would look like a scoreboard,

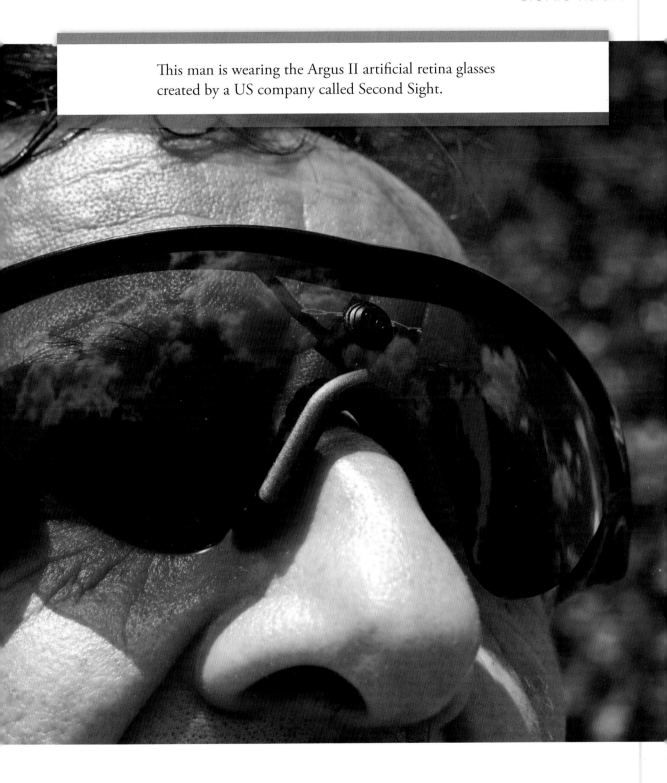

This man is wearing the Argus II artificial retina glasses created by a US company called Second Sight.

where numbers or simple pictures are made from dots of light." The next-generation bionic vision prototype will use a grid of one hundred electrodes, according to the researchers, providing enough clarity for the wearer to navigate and identify faces.

TOWARD CLEARER VISION

Perfecting bionic vision has required advances in many areas. Medically, the microsurgery required to implant the device in the eye is delicate. A tiny incision is made in the back of the eyeball. Then the device is placed behind the retina. The approach, called ab-externo ("from outside"), reduces the chance of injuring eye tissue. "Most of the device rides on the eyeball, with only the fine electrodes intruding into the eye itself," says Kelly.

Electronics for the device require careful engineering. For example, the electrodes may only deliver a small amount of electricity. This prevents damage to delicate eye tissue. This voltage must also be customized. For example, patients blind for a long time may require a slightly higher voltage.

The human body is also a surprisingly harsh environment for electronic parts. "In our design, the microchip is hermetically sealed [airtight] inside a titanium case to protect it from the body's moisture," says Kelly. For the bionic eye to last, materials must be biocompatible. That means they don't hurt the body, and aren't hurt by the body. "Our goal is a bionic eye that can operate inside the body for ten years," says Kelly.

A PRACTICAL MIRACLE

Real bionic vision won't look much like what you might see on TV or in movies. And Kelly warns that its clarity won't approach normal vision either. "Our goal is providing enough visual sense of the world to help restore a patient's basic mobility and independence," he says. Patients will see in black and white, since adding color would prove even more complex.

The system is also designed to assist only patients who could once see. "Our minds learn all things by experience," says Kelly. "In babies, the visual systems in the brain develop through experience." But the brains of patients who are blind from birth do not have that experience to rely on, making this type of bionic vision unsuitable for them.

It makes you realize just how amazing the human eye is. Even with all the technology we have today, it is hard to replicate!

GLOSSARY

cone A cone-shaped cell located in the retina of the eye that contains a pigment sensitive to red, green, or blue light.

cornea The transparent outer coating of the eyeball.

deficient Lacking.

electrode A conductor through which electricity enters or leaves an object, substance, or area.

iris The colored part of the eye.

lens A curved, often transparent, substance that concentrates or disperses light.

photoreceptor A specialized cell, such as a cone or rod in an eye, that responds to light.

pixel One of many small image-forming units of a digital image.

prototype A model on which later stages are based.

retina The light-sensitive membrane lining the inner eyeball and connected by the optic nerve to the brain.

rod A long cell that detects light and darkness.

synesthete A person who has synesthesia, which means he or she experience senses with more than one sense.

thalamus The area of the brain that sends sensory impulses to the cerebral cortex, which is responsible for higher brain functions.

visual cortex The part of the cerebral cortex that processes signals from the eyes.

voltage The measurement of the energy contained within an electric field, or an electric circuit, at a given point.

BOOKS

Huddle, Rusty, and Jennifer Viegas. *The Eye in 3D*. New York, NY: Rosen, 2016.

Sheen, Barbara. *Artificial Eyes*. Chicago, IL: Norwood House Press, 2016.

Silverstein, Alvin, Virginia Silverstein, and Laura Silverstein Nunn. *Handy Health Guide to Your Eyes*. Berkeley Heights, NJ: Enslow Publishers, 2013.

Stamps, Caroline. *The Human Body*. London: DK Books, 2013.

WEBSITES

KidsHealth, Your Eyes
kidshealth.org/en/kids/eyes.html
Learn more about the human eye and how it works.

NEI for Kids
nei.nih.gov/kids
The National Eye Institute website provides facts, safety and health tips, fun eye tricks, optical illusions, and more.

Neuroscience for Kids, The Eye
faculty.washington.edu/chudler/bigeye.html
Dive deeper into information about the anatomy of the human eye.